ALLEN PHOTOGR

C000156528

HARNESSING UP

CONTENTS

PUTTING ON THE FULL COLLAR

A full collar shown hanging upside down with the hame tugs tied up to the rein terrets to prevent them swinging about when they are being fitted to the collar. The top hame strap is being undone.

The collar, with the hames removed, is stretched by the assistant using her knee to widen the collar before placing it over the horse's head.

AUTHORS' TIP

A horse with a large head, wide between the eyes, and a thin narrow neck, should have an open-top collar. This is fastened at the top with a housing strap which enables the collar to be placed round the horse's neck without having to put it over the horse's head. This type of collar is also known as a posting collar. Care should be taken to see that the housing strap does not stretch as this can allow the horse's neck to be pinched by the opening top.

The collar is put over the horse's head upside down – the widest part of the collar being the throat – thus preventing damage to the horse's eyes. The horse is shown wearing a webbing halter. If a headcollar is used it is all too easy to tear the lining of the collar with the tongue of the headcollar buckle.

▼ The assistant pointing to the tongue of the headcollar buckle.

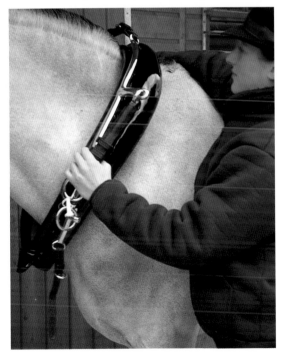

◄ The collar has been taken back to rest on the horse's shoulders and the hames are being placed over the collar.

◄Fastening the top hame strap prior to turning the collar the right way up.

▲The collar being turned over on the horse's neck. First, the collar is taken forward to just behind the horse's ears and is then turned with the lay of the mane. It is then eased back into the correct position.

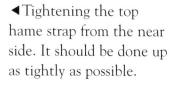

◄Tightening the top hame strap from the near side. It should be done up as tightly as possible.

The collar in position with the traces neatly rolled up.

> **AUTHORS' TIP**
>
> When driving using a full collar the whole safety of the turnout depends on the strength of the two hame straps. It is vitally important that they should be sound and strong. If a hame chain is used instead of a bottom hame strap it should be steel, not brass which will break. If either of the hame straps should break the hames will come off the collar allowing the horse to come out of the shafts with disastrous results.

PUTTING ON THE SINGLE-HARNESS SADDLE

The saddle laid over the horse's back with the back strap and crupper dock attached. The dock is a closed one, so the horse's tail has been folded prior to being put through the crupper dock. It is important to remember to smooth the tail hairs after fitting the crupper dock because tail hairs caught up in the dock can make a horse kick.

▼▶ The saddle girth being fastened.

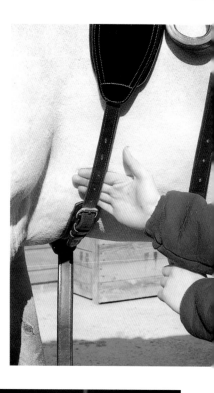

▶ The fastened girth. A hand between the horse's side and the girth shows the correct adjustment. The girth of a harness saddle should never be pulled up tightly as with a riding saddle. If it is, a girth gall can be caused by the backward and forward thrust of the shafts through the tugs when a vehicle is in movement.

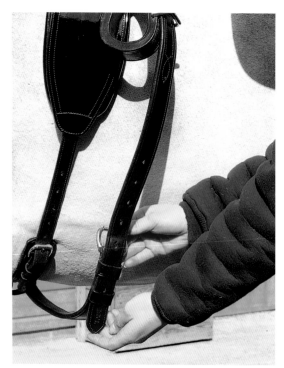

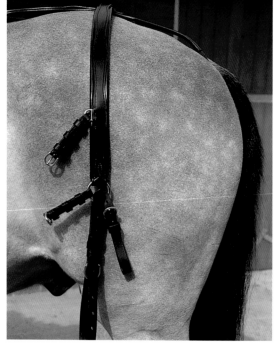

The back band being slotted through the keepers of the belly band, prior to putting to.

The breeching shown lying over the horse's quarters before being fastened to the loin strap.

The loin strap of the breeching is being pushed through the slot in the back strap.

Buckling the loin strap to the seat of breeching.

The breeching correctly fitted and the breeching strap and trace bearer in place.

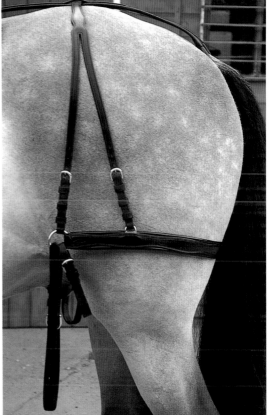

THE REINS

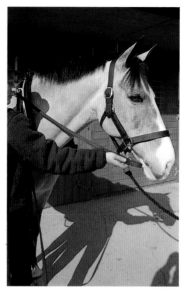

The reins, showing the billet and buckle on the hand pieces of the reins *(above)*. Slotting the reins through the rein terrets on the saddle and collar *(centre)*. Measuring the reins from the collar terret to the horse's mouth to assess the correct length before putting up the reins *(above right)*.

Fastening the bit-billet end of the reins to the collar terret to keep the reins out of harm's way prior to putting on the bridle.

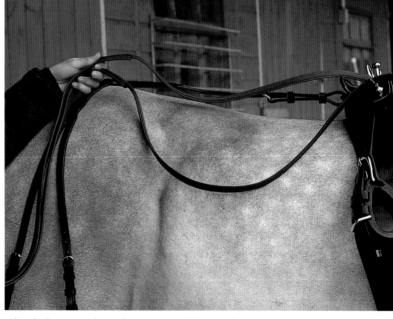

The left rein placed on top of the right prior to putting up the reins.

▶ The reins folded in half before being slotted through the off-side saddle terret.

▼ The end of the reins doubled and passed through the loop of the reins in the terret and then pulled firm.

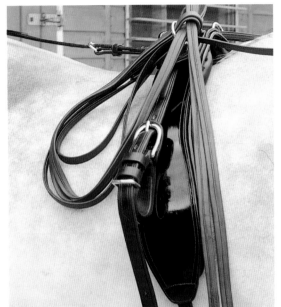

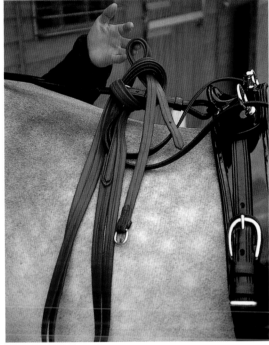

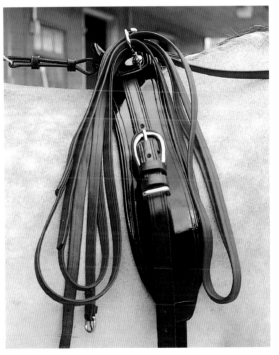

▲ Another way of putting up the reins. The reins are doubled around the crupper back strap and then the doubled end slotted back through the reins and pulled tight.

◀ A very simple method of putting up the reins. Place the left rein on top of the right, fold the reins in half and then slot them through the off-side saddle terret.

PUTTING ON THE BRIDLE

Putting on the bridle, asking the horse to open his mouth and accept the bit.

The bridle in place. The reins shown fastened to the rough cheek of the Liverpool bit.

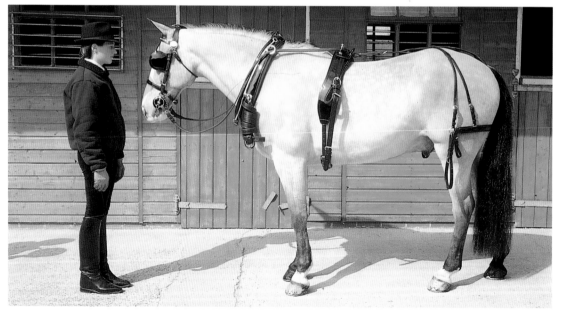

The horse shown fully harnessed, ready to be put to.

REIN ADJUSTMENTS ON A LIVERPOOL BIT

Smooth or plain cheek. This is the least severe adjustment with little or no curb action. The disadvantage of this adjustment is that the reins tend to slide up into the top of the bit ring, which pulls the bit backwards into the corners of the horse's mouth rendering the curb chain useless.

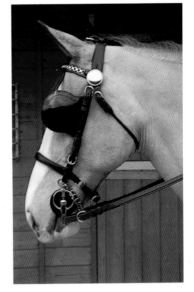

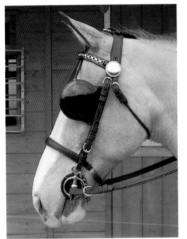

Rough cheek. The rein billet is attached around the cheek piece below the mouth piece. As a result of this attachment, the action of the bit is applied to the horse's poll, nose and chin groove.

Bottom bar. This should not be resorted to unless the horse has a *very* hard mouth, and only then if a kinder way of dealing with the problem cannot be found.

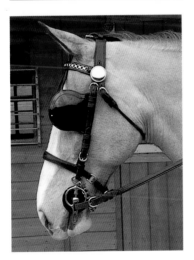

Top bar. Owing to the increased leverage against the cheek piece of the bit, the action of the bit is more severe than with the rough cheek attachment.

AUTHORS' TIP

The Liverpool driving bit shown has the top-bar slot within the bit ring. This is a milder rein setting than when the top-bar slot is set below the bit ring. In some instances a more satisfactory rough-cheek rein attachment can be achieved by using this top-bar slot with a looser curb chain.

PUTTING ON A BREAST COLLAR

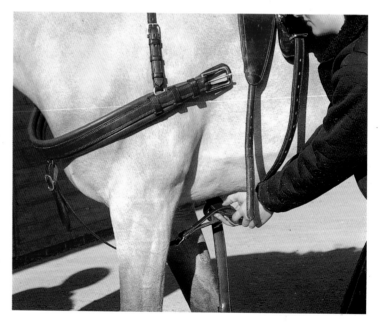

▲ The collar held upside down, with the false martingale already attached, prior to being placed over the horse's head.

▲▶ The collar is placed over the horse's head and then turned the right way up.

▶ The collar in place and the girth being slotted through the false martingale.

PUTTING ON A SADDLE WITH THE BREECHING ATTACHED

◄ The saddle shown with the breeching already attached.

▼◄ Placing the saddle on the horse's back

▼ The saddle in position and the seat of the breeching being passed over the horse's rump.

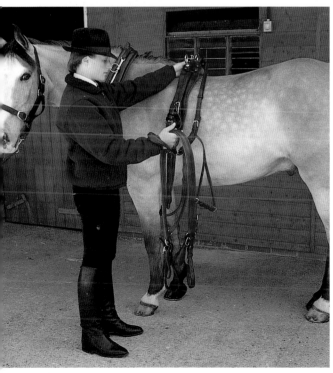

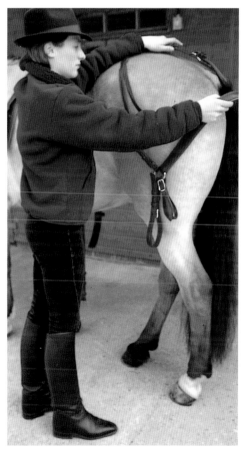

▼The saddle girth fastened with room for a hand's breadth between it and the horse's side.

▼The crupper with an opening dock ready for fitting.

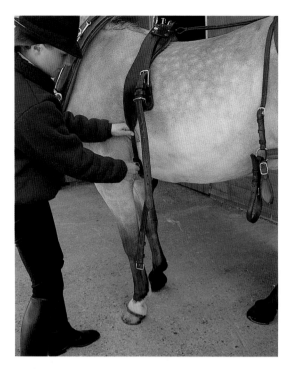

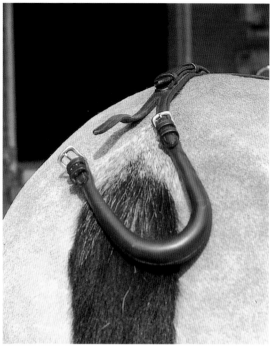

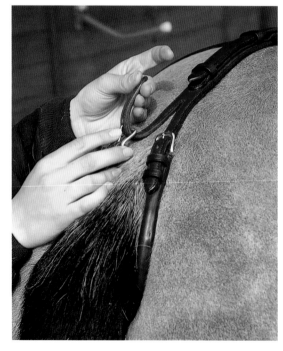

▲The crupper dock being put under the horse's tail. Care is being taken to ensure that all the tail hairs are lying smoothly.

▲ Buckling up the dock.

FITTING OF THE FULL AND BREAST COLLAR

▶ A hand slipped between the horse's neck and the neck of the collar, showing that it is not too tight and pinching the horse.

> **AUTHORS' TIP**
>
> Too wide a collar will rock from side to side causing a sore neck which is difficult to heal.

▼ A hand's breadth betwwen the horse's gullet and the collar, showing that the collar is big enough not to throttle the horse when in draft.

> **AUTHORS' TIP**
>
> Too long a collar will slide up and back when the horse is in draft, particularly going up hill, thus pressing on the horse's windpipe and throttling him. Too short a collar will strangle the horse. It is always advisable to use a false martingale with a full collar as this helps to keep the collar in place.

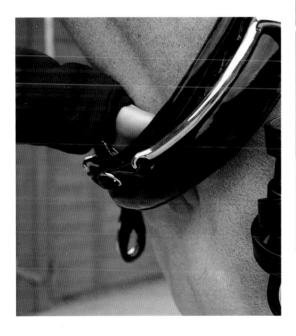

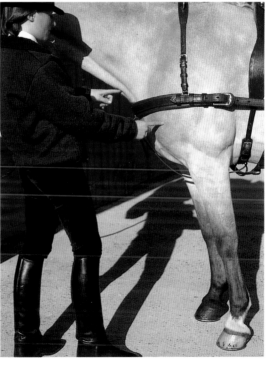

The breast collar should lie approximately halfway between the horse's windpipe and point of shoulder.

FITTING OF THE SINGLE-HARNESS SADDLE

A well-padded saddle with a good clearance where the arch of the saddle crosses the horse's backbone.

> **AUTHORS' TIP**
>
> An ill-fitting single-harness saddle, or one that is in need of reflocking, can cause severe pain and discomfort to the horse because the weight of the vehicle will be taken on the horse's backbone. The crupper back-strap dee rubbing on the backbone soon causes a bad gall.

FITTING THE CRUPPER BACK STRAP

A hand's breadth shows the correct fitting; neither too tight nor too loose.

FITTING OF THE BREECHING

The seat of the breeching lies horizontally in line with the horse's stifle joint, approximately halfway between the horse's dock and hock.

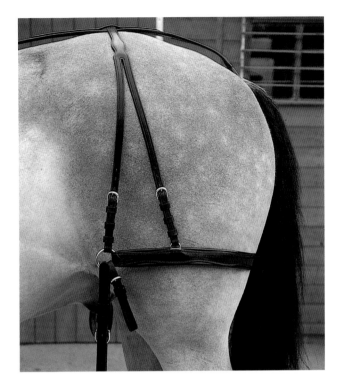

FITTING THE BRIDLE

▶ The bridle is shown from the front to demonstrate the correct fit of the winkers. The eyes should be in the centre of the winkers which must not press on the eyes or eyelashes.

▶▶ The correct fitting of the browband; it is long enough to prevent the pinching of the base of the ears by the headstall.

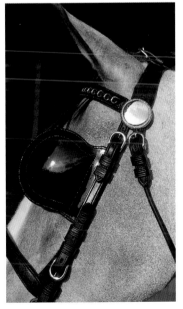

The throatlatch adjusted to allow a hand's breadth between it and the horse's cheek. When the horse flexes his neck he will not be choked by the throatlatch being too tight.

The noseband adjusted to allow the insertion of two fingers between it and the horse's jaw.

The curb chain – twisted until it is flat – allowing two fingers to be inserted between it and the horse's chin groove.

PUTTING THE HORSE TO THE VEHICLE

The vehicle ready on the stand before putting the horse to.

AUTHORS' TIP

One of the authors found, by experience, that it was best *not* to put the whip in the socket as by doing so it was extremely easy to break a whip stick. She had the whip sockets removed from all of her vehicles for this reason.

▼ Bringing the vehicle up to the horse and warning the horse it is coming by gently placing a hand on his quarters. N.B. The traces have been unwound and laid across the horse's back, and the breeching straps have been undone.

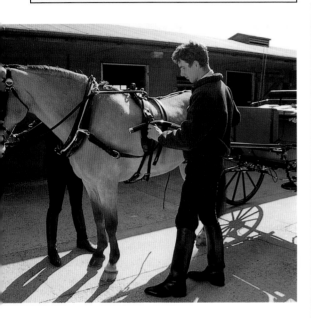

▲ Slotting the shafts through the tugs with an assistant on each side.

◄◄ Putting the traces through the trace bearers before fastening them to the swingle tree or splinter bar trace hooks.

◄ Hooking the crew eye of the trace to the swingle tree hook.

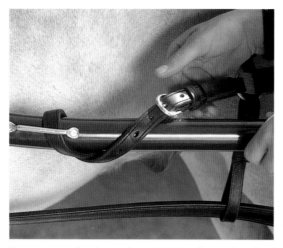

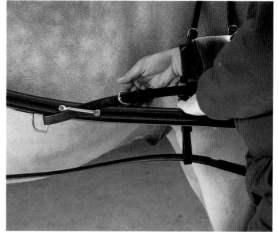

Fastening the breeching strap through the breeching dee on the shaft.

Fastening the breeching strap to the under-shaft dee, then passing it up through the outside breeching dee. An alternative method of fastening.

AUTHORS' TIP

If the breeching strap is fastened to the under-shaft dee alone, care should be taken to see that this is made of steel. It should also be secured to the shaft in such a manner that it cannot pull out. Slotting the breeching strap through the shaft dee gives added protection.

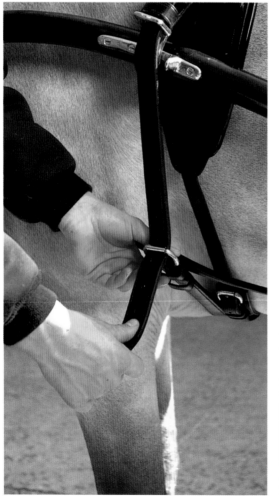

Fastening the belly band to the back band.

AUTHORS' TIP

The belly band shown in the photograph is not long enough. To be correct, the buckle should reach the bottom edge of the saddle flap when fastened. There should be at least two fingers distance between the fastened girth and belly band when the horse has been put to.

IMPORTANT HORSE AND VEHICLE CHECKS

CORRECT FITTING OF HORSE TO VEHICLE

Put the horse to on a flat and level piece of ground. When the body of the vehicle is parallel to the ground the shaft tug stops should lie on the widest part of the saddle panel (*see first photo on page 22*). There should be approximately 18 inches (45.7 cm) clearance between the hindmost part of the horse and the foremost part of the vehicle. The shaft tip should lie approximately level with the horse's point of shoulder and there should be a gap of approximately two inches between the shafts and the horse's rib cage.

CORRECT HARNESSING OF HORSE TO VEHICLE

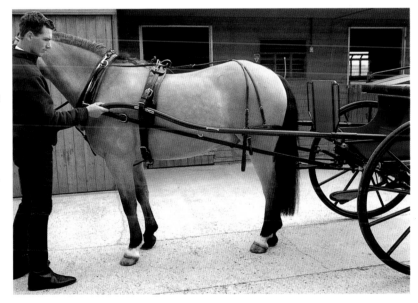

Having first attached the traces to the swingle tree, gently push the carriage backwards so that the traces are in draft. The back band and tugs should lie centrally on the swell of the saddle panel, with approximately one inch (2.5 cm) between the tug and the tug stop.

▶ The tug and back band lying centrally on the saddle.

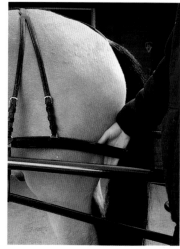

▶▶ Having attached the breeching straps, and the horse is standing in draft, there should be one hand's breadth between the horse's quarters and the seat of breeching.

To assess that the breeching is correctly adjusted, gently pull the vehicle forwards until the horse is seated in the breeching, thereby holding the vehicle back. The breeching should engage before the shaft tugs take any weight and the tugs should not be pushed forward of the saddle panel. (*see top left photo*)

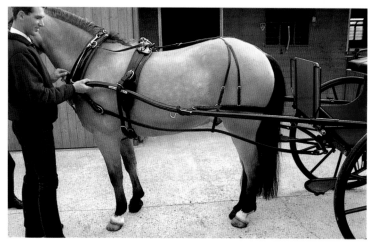

CORRECT VEHICLE BALANCE

If the vehicle is correctly balanced when the driver is up, there should be a minimal weight of approximately two pounds in the hand of the assistant when the shafts are lifted slightly.

AUTHORS' TIP

A vehicle that is built with a sliding seat is very much easier to balance than one with a seat that is incorporated into the body of the vehicle, as with a gig and some modern carriages.

When a correctly balanced two-wheeled vehicle is moving at trot, the tug buckles should gently open and close with the movement of the shafts. The shafts should also appear to float in the tugs.

AUTHORS' TIP

The photograph shows a spares kit suitable for the show ring. For everyday purposes the following items should be carried: sharp knife, leather punch, boot lace, simple first-aid kit, paper, pen, a pound coin, headcollar and lead rope. Your name, address and telephone number should be carefully visible on your carriage.

Spare Equipment should always be carried on the vehicle in case of emergencies.

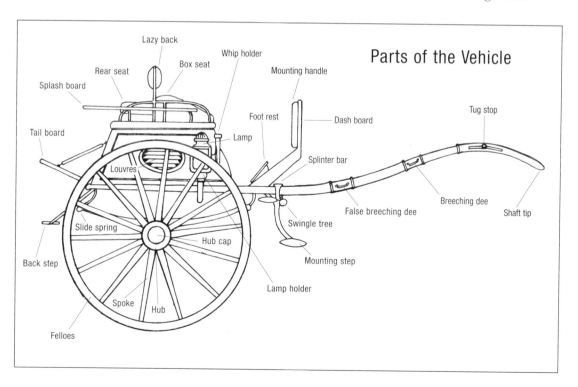

Parts of the Vehicle

Lazy back
Whip holder
Box seat
Rear seat
Mounting handle
Splash board
Tug stop
Foot rest
Dash board
Tail board
Lamp
Louvres
Splinter bar
Slide spring
Breeching dee
Hub cap
False breeching dee
Shaft tip
Back step
Swingle tree
Mounting step
Lamp holder
Spoke
Hub
Felloes

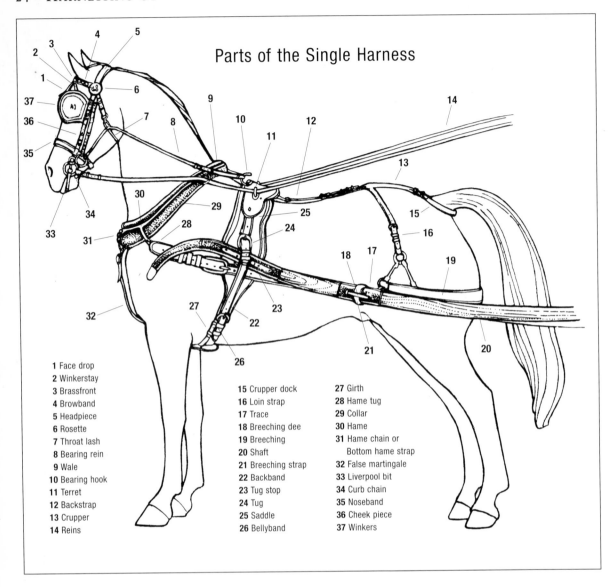

Parts of the Single Harness

1 Face drop
2 Winkerstay
3 Brassfront
4 Browband
5 Headpiece
6 Rosette
7 Throat lash
8 Bearing rein
9 Wale
10 Bearing hook
11 Terret
12 Backstrap
13 Crupper
14 Reins

15 Crupper dock
16 Loin strap
17 Trace
18 Breeching dee
19 Breeching
20 Shaft
21 Breeching strap
22 Backband
23 Tug stop
24 Tug
25 Saddle
26 Bellyband

27 Girth
28 Hame tug
29 Collar
30 Hame
31 Hame chain or
    Bottom hame strap
32 False martingale
33 Liverpool bit
34 Curb chain
35 Noseband
36 Cheek piece
37 Winkers

ACKNOWLEDGEMENTS

Dounhurst Mr Mac, Nessie Coulton BHSAI,
Henrik Hoper Nilsen

British Library Cataloguing-in-Publication Data.
A catalogue record for this book is available from the
British Library

ISBN 0.85131.657.3

© J. A. Allen & Co. Ltd., 1996
First published in 1979 by J. A. Allen & Co. Ltd.
Reprinted 1981, 1984, 1986, 1989, 1993:
Revised edition 1996

Published in Great Britain in 1996 by
J. A. Allen & Company Limited,
1 Lower Grosvenor Place, Buckingham Palace Road,
London, SW1W OEL

Illustrations by Maggie Raynor
Design and Typesetting by Paul Saunders
Printed in Hong Kong by Midas Printing Ltd.